Blogging For Nincompoops

How To Make Money Blogging For Profit,
A Beginners Guide

(Blogging For Income Series, Book 1)

Walter Gruebenschticker

© Copyright 2019 - All rights reserved.

In no way is it legal to reproduce, duplicate, or transmit any part of this document by either electronic means or in printed format. Recording of this publication is strictly prohibited, and any storage of this document is not allowed without written permission from the publisher.

This publication is geared towards providing exact and reliable information in regard to the topics and issues covered. The publication is not a substitute for legal, tax, financial or professional advice. If such advice is necessary, a practiced individual in the profession should be consulted.

The publisher makes no guarantees regarding income as a result of applying the information contained in this document, and any liability regarding inattention or otherwise, by any usage or abuse of any policies, processes, or directions contained within is the solitary and utter responsibility of the recipient reader, and as such, for all intents and purposes, this document is to be considered as being "for entertainment purposes only." The reader should always seek the advice of a professional when making any medical, legal, tax, financial, or business decisions.

Under no circumstances will any legal responsibility or blame be held against the publisher for any reparation, damages, medical issues, or monetary loss due to the information herein, either directly or indirectly.

Any trademarks or brands mentioned in this publication are without any consent, permission, or backing of the trademark owner.

All trademarks and brands within this book are used only for the purposes of clarification, and are owned by the owners themselves, and not affiliated with this publication.

All copyrights not held by the publisher, are owned by the respective authors.

Introduction

If you're new to the world of blogging, then you're in the right place, as this book is going to show you exactly what you need to do to get started blogging. And even more importantly this book is going to show you how you should be setting up your blog so that you can earn an income from it.

The reality is that blogging is not that hard. Nearly anyone can start one. However, most people think it's hard to set up a blog. And as a result, most people don't start one.

So if you're having doubts, all you need to do is get it out of your head that it's hard to start a blog, and approach it with an 'I CAN DO IT!' attitude, because the reality is that YOU CAN DO IT!

Don't get me wrong though, it's not easy to start a blog. It takes dedication because you'll have to write blog posts regularly which amounts to a lot of hard work. However, if you're okay with the writing aspect, and if you're okay with the hard work. Then this book will provide you with the plan that you'll need to make this blogging thing happen.

Therefore, let's jump right in and get your blog created! See you in Chapter 1!

Table of Contents

Introduction	4
Chapter 1: Deciding What To Blog About	8
Chapter 2: Pen Names	11
Chapter 3: Building The Blog	13
Chapter 4: Making Blog Posts	18
Chapter 5: Continuous Learning	22
Chapter 6: Posting	26
Chapter 7: Images	29
Chapter 8: Blogger's Block	31
Chapter 9: Introduction to AM	34
Chapter 10: FTC	39
Chapter 11: Ergonomics	41
Chapter 12: Traffic	44
Chapter 13: Google Webmasters	48
Chapter 14: Guest Posting	51
Chapter 15: Email Marketing	54

Chapter 16: Blogger Lifestyle   **60**

Chapter 17: End   **64**

Chapter 1: Deciding What To Blog About

Okay, you've made it to Chapter 1, so that means you're ready to start a blog. Well, congratulations, because most people don't make it this far. You're a special one you are!

Right, so before we can get into what you need to do to actually create your blog and monetize it, we, first of all, need to figure out what exactly your blog is going to be about. Now if you already know what you want to blog about, then great, then you don't need to read any further, you can just jump right ahead to Chapter 2. However, for the rest of you, you're going to need to stick around here in Chapter 1 so that we can find a good niche for you.

What is a niche you ask? Well, a niche is an area of interest. There are many niches, such as Tennis, Horseback Riding, Music Production, Engineering, Role Playing Games, Chess, Apple Juice, Microwave Ovens, Nail Polish, and the list goes on and on.

When we're deciding on a niche, the two most important factors would be:

1. That you are passionate about it!

2. That it's something that you can write a nearly infinite number of blog-posts on!

So you're going to need to think, and you're going to need to come up with something that matches the above-stated criteria.

If you're drawing a blank and can't think of anything, then I would recommend getting out a piece of paper and a pen and making a list of things that you like, and then choose something off of your list. You must have some kind of hobby or something that you like to do!

What's that you say? You say you don't have any hobbies and you don't like to do anything? Oh my, well then you're going to need to step away from this book and look around and find something that you like.

How about pancakes? Do you like pancakes? Well,

how about a pancake blog? Not so much into breakfast foods? Well then, what kinds of foods do you eat? You must eat I would imagine. Really? You don't eat anything at all? Hmmm, you're a tough one. Well, you must drink at least? If you didn't consume some kind of liquid refreshment, then you wouldn't live very long, so how about a blog about bottled water? You don't like that idea, huh? Well, that's good, because I didn't like that idea either.

You say you just want to blog about your life, like a diary. Well, that's a niche too, you could do that. However, if your blog is more focused on one specific thing that you do that you like, then it's going to be much easier to build a following.

Anyway, it's up to you, you must have chosen something by now. So onward, to Chapter 2!

What, you're still thinking? Huh? Well, then take your time at it I suppose, because we need to move on to Chapter 2 now. When you come up with something, we'll all be waiting for you in Chapter 2, see you there!

Chapter 2: Pen Names

The next thing you're going to have to decide is whether you want to write your blog under your name, or whether you want to write it under a pen name.

I myself run multiple blogs, and run them all under pen names. And my reason for this is quite simple, it's because I don't want people to recognize me everywhere I go. Now, fame is desirable by many, but it has its drawbacks, such as paparazzi following you, and not being able to drink your coffee in a cafe and write your blog without hoards of fans rushing your table pushing each other out of the way to get your autograph.

If you're okay with the drawbacks of fame, then by all means, feel free to blog under your own name. However, if you value your privacy, then a pen name might be a better way for you to go.

Of course, putting your name and your face on your blog has the advantage of your following having a feeling like they can more easily connect with you.

Though, ultimately, it's not your name or what you look like that's going to decide how successful your blog becomes. Rather, what decides the success of your blog is how valuable the content you put out is to your niche. Keep that in mind.

Therefore, as you can imagine, I for one am a big fan of pen names. I have all my blogs written under different pen names, and I also write numerous books under pen names, including this one. And which route you ultimately decided to go is totally and completely up to you.

If you do go the pen name route, then do make sure that your pen name is not a name that is already being used by anyone with a blog, or by anyone famous for that matter, or you could get sued for it. To find out if the pen name that you want is already in use, it's as simple as doing a Google search. And you'll want to follow up that Google search with a trademark search just to be sure it's not trademarked. I'll show you where you can do a trademark search in the next chapter. See you there!

Chapter 3: Building The Blog

If you build it, followers will come!

Most people who get into blogging with the intent of turning it into a career usually fall flat on their face when it comes to building it. They think it's going to be all technical and they freak out and stop dead in their tracks, never to blog a single word.

However, that doesn't have to be you, as long as you follow the instructions in this chapter.

The first thing you're going to need when building your blog is hosting. If you already have hosting, then fine. However, if you don't have hosting and don't know what you're doing with hosting, then I'd like to recommend a host that you can find at the following link:

BloggerBlogger.com/Basics

I'm giving you a link and not a hosting provider name, because the best deal on hosting is subject to change, so I try to keep that page always updated with what the best deal around is.

You just go there and click the big green button that says "Get The Best Price On Hosting" and then you should see a red or orange button that says "Get Started Now" or "Get Plan" or something to that extent.

And it should take you to a page where you can enter a domain name.

This is where you want to try and type in different names with a dot come after them, and try to find a domain name that isn't already taken.

Your domain name will also be your blog name, so it should be related to your niche. Don't think too hard about it, because domain names are not as important as they used to be. Most important is that your domain is relevant to your niche, that you like it as your blog name, and that it's not already taken.

One more thing I should say is just because your domain name isn't taken doesn't mean the name you want isn't trademarked, if you find a good name that isn't taken, you'll want to check the name in a trademark database. The one I like to use can be found at:

Wipo.Int/BrandDB

Once you come up with something, meaning the domain name is not taken, and also that no one has trademarked the name, go ahead and purchase hosting. Yes, we do have to purchase hosting to start a blog. Everyone with a successful blog has hosting. There isn't really a way to get around that aspect of things. However, it's going to be well worth the investment, since you'll be able to get a blog up that you can monetize and customize, trust me on this. Also, the hosting I've recommended at the mentioned link is one of the cheapest hosting providers around that gives you the most value for your dollar, which is exactly why I'm recommending them. Sure you can shop around for something else, but it's unlikely you're going to find a better deal with more value than that, as I've already done the hundreds of hours of research shopping around for you, so that you don't have to. But should you find something better that I didn't know about, well be sure to let me know in that case and I may update my page with your pick! You can contact me anytime at:

BloggerBlogger.com/Contact

Once you have hosting, your next step is going to be to install WordPress. If you have any trouble installing WordPress, then just ask your host's support what to do, as it's their job to assist you in getting WordPress installed.

Once WordPress is installed on your host, then you're going to need to log into your Admin panel with your username and password, something you should have gotten when you installed WordPress.

Next, you need to choose a Theme, so what you do is, you look on the left side of your WordPress dashboard and you look for the word "Appearance," you hover over that, and this will cause a menu to pop up which has the word "Themes" in it. So you click on "Themes."

You then should look for a button that says "Add New," and this will take you to a page where you can look at many different kinds of free themes.

Take your time and look through all the different themes there and choose one. You can always change your theme later, so don't get all hung up on choosing the perfect theme, just pick one that looks good enough, and later on you can analyze it further and try some other themes.

Once you've chosen a theme, you'll want to look for an "Install" button. I know you can find it.

Now that your chosen theme is installed, you want to find and click the "Activate" button. And your blog has been built!

Excellent job! Now we're ready to make some blog posts, see you in the next chapter!

Chapter 4: Making Blog Posts

Okay, so now you have Hosting, you have WordPress installed, you have your Theme activated, and so we're ready to get our hands dirty and make some blog posts! Great!

Before we do that, I'm going to ask you to go over to the black bar on the left side of your WordPress dashboard and hover over "Settings," which should cause a menu to pop up, and click on the word "Permalinks" in that menu.

Once you're there, make sure to click the checkbox next to "Post name," and then click the blue "Save Changes" button at the bottom of the screen. We only need to do that once ever. What we just did was basically make sure that the name of our blog posts will show up in the URL (uniform resource locator) bar, so they can be easily shared by your followers. If that doesn't make sense to you now, don't worry about it, as long as you followed the instructions, you're fine.

Next, we look on the left side of our WordPress dashboard for the word "Posts," and we hover over it, which will cause a menu to pop up. We then click "Add New" in that menu. And it will then take is to a page where we're ready to write our first blog post!

Are you excited? Well, you should be! If you're not excited, then stop reading this book and jump up and down or something, and get excited! Because I don't want you completing these next steps without being excited, because writing your first blog post is an exciting moment, it means you've crossed the threshold between normal internet user and blogger! Once you do this you're going to be a blogger, so you'd better darn well be excited about this!

So at the top, you'll see a field where you're going to write in your first blog post's title. You can write anything you want here. If you don't know what to write, then how about, "My First Blog Post." It doesn't matter so much what you write at this point, as we're going to make more blog posts later.

We're just trying to get you acclimated to things at this moment, so it's probably best to just write something simple.

Below the title field, you should see a bigger field, and that's where your blog post body goes. Now, don't write your body text yet, let's stick an image in there, like every pro blogger should.

So you look for an "Add Media" button above the body text field and click on it.

It will take you to another area called the Add Media page. At the top, you will see 2 tabs. If you have a nice photo on your computer you'd like to use then click on the left tab, which should say "Upload Files," then click the button in the center of the screen which says "Select Files" and then you choose your image, and press "Open." And then finally you click the blue "Insert Into Post" button in the lower right.

Then go back to the body field and make sure in the tab to the upper right of it that the "Visual" tab is selected. Then click in the body field below your image and write your blog post. Just writing one customized email, how to set up an SSL for your blog, and how to navigate your host's dashboard and do a myriad of other things. Especially, setting up customized email and SSL is critical, so you'll want to get on this.

The process for every host will be different, so don't worry about how things are done on other people's hosts. You instead want to focus on learning everything about your host that you possibly can.

Don't be hard on your hosts support if they don't immediately understand your questions or take a lot of time to respond. As support often has to deal with many customers at once; it's a hard job. Also, these support people think like programmers, not like regular people, so the fact that they even speak English and not purely techno-babble is pretty good. Just be patient with them and polite, and you should eventually get the answers you need. After all, they don't want you constantly bugging them, so it's a win-win situation for both you and your host if they can resolve your issues.

Learn WordPress

WordPress is another beast that's going to require further learning on your part.

Sure, if you can write blog posts as we've taught you in this book, that's basically all you need. However, there's going to come a time where you're going to want to install a plugin or do some other thing, so learning WordPress a little every day should be your priority.

No, you don't need a WordPress book. Learning WordPress should be on the computer. You basically want to play around with each feature and try to understand it and see how it affects your blog. If there is something you want to do, you just type the question in your search engine and you should be able to get your answer somewhere in the first few results that pop up.

This is how everyone who gets good at blogging learns WordPress, we type questions in our search engine. And if you do a little each day before you know it you'll be a master at WordPress. It's not that hard to master WordPress, it can be done in a few weeks if you spend a little bit of time each day on it, or even in a weekend if you spend 2 days straight on it. It's not rocket science.

And that's really all you need to focus on besides actually blogging, learning your host's system and learning WordPress continuously. As you get better at both, things will start to make a lot more sense to you.

And that's really all you'll need to spend your time learning. Yes, there are some other things you'll also need to add to your continuous learning regimen, and we'll get to those soon enough.

Chapter 6: Posting

Basically, what you want to do is to make blog posts regularly. This means you want to post once a week, or twice a week, or three times a week, or every day for that matter, if you can!

You know your schedule better than anyone else, so you want to choose posting days, and on those days your number one most important thing you should be working on is writing good, high-quality blog posts with images in them.

Let's say Wednesday and Thursday are your blog posting days. Well, then on Wednesday and Thursday, you're not allowed to do anything or go out anywhere until you get one blog post done.

On other days when your not writing blog posts, you should be thinking about something good that you can write about for your next blog post, and note down those ideas when they come to you on your blog posting idea list, so when your next blog posting day comes, you already have an assortment of topics to choose from.

So how do you write blog posts? Well, you basically sit down in a chair at a desk in front of your computer, or it could be in a cafe with your laptop, and you sip on some kind of drink, whatever you like, I like coffee, and you start writing and you finish one blog post no matter how long or short it is.

You want to strive to really get into writing blog posts, so that time just passes without you noticing and by the end of your posting session a masterpiece came out of you.

It should take you no more than 2 to 3 hours to write a blog post. And make sure you edit your blog posts well too, as readers don't like to read blog posts with a lot of mistakes in them. Regardless though, by the end of 2 or 3 hours, you should spend maybe 30 min to an hour to review what you've got. It may be 500 words, it may be 3,000 words, whatever it is, is fine! Then you hit that publish button, and whamo! Another blog post done!

As long as you always post on your posting days, you'll have a large assortment of blog posts up before you know it as the weeks and months roll by, and your blog will grow by leaps and bounds.

It's really important to stick to your posting schedule. If you fail to post on your posting days, it could spell death for your blog, as skipping posting days is a hard habit to recover from and most blogs die as a result of someone thinking: I'll just skip my posting day just this once, and then they never post again.

You need to write your blog posts on your posting days no matter what! Not before, not after. Write your blog posts on your posting days and that's it! And as long as you do that, you've got a blog!

Chapter 7: Images

Some of you may be wondering, where do I get images?

Well, the best place to get them is to take them yourself. If you have a cell phone, you have a camera on it, and if you've never used it before, well now is a good time to figure it out. It's mostly point and click, so it's not hard to actually take photos, but what you have to think about is what kinds of photos you need to take for your blog.

In fact, every time you note down a topic that you're going to write a blog post about, you should already be thinking about what kind of image would look best in the blog post, and where do I have to go to take that photo?

Now, if you don't want to run around shooting photos for your blog, then there is another way. And that way is called stock photo sites. Many of these stock photos sites have a cost, but there are a number of free ones. And you can basically just type "stock photos" in your search engine, and you'll find a bunch of stock photo sites that way.

Very important though is the license of each photo. You want to read the terms and conditions of the site, and make sure you understand how the license to the photo works. If you're planning to monetize your blog, and you should be planning to monetize your blog, otherwise why would you have picked up this book? Then you need to make sure that it's okay to use whatever stock photo you want to use for commercial use.

Whatever you do, do not just steal images off other websites. Because you'd think that they'd never notice, but they will notice, and you can be sued for it, and have to pay out a whole lot of money, so you definitely don't want to do that!

Really, the simplest way to run things without having to worry about licenses is to just take your own photos. However, if you're dead against that, then stock photo sites would be the next way to go.

And that's pretty much all there is to images.

Chapter 8: Blogger's Block

Now it might happen that you're sitting at your chair, at your desk trying to write a blog post, and no words come out. Nothing comes out. So what do you do in this case?

Well, this situation can happen, and this is called blogger's block. And should it happen, you force a post out. I don't care if it's below par, and only about 200 words, you force something out of that magnificent mind of yours, whatever it is!

You see, when you're sitting there and nothing comes out, a battle is being waged in your mind. One side of our brain is saying, " I don't know what to write, I just want to vegetate."

And the other side of your brain is saying, "Nothing will come out, I'm freaking out! I have to post on my posting day!"

You can choose which side of your mind you listen

to, and the choice you make determines which side of your brain will win the battle. If you win these battles enough times, blogger's block will become an issue that seldom occurs.

So don't give into blogger's block, just power through! Just sit there and think, and think and think and think, and look at your hands and tell them to write, scream at them to write.

You want those fingers of yours to dance on the keyboard, and if they're not dancing, then you have to get strict with them. Now, if you're in a cafe, don't disturb others by actually yelling and screaming at your hands aloud or people might think you're a looney.

Your hands have telepathic ability to hear what your mind is thinking, so just scream at them silently, and give them menacing stares. That usually will do the trick!

If you're persistent, your hands will eventually give in, and start to write.

Now, don't put them in a bad ergonomic position or anything, or it could lead to one of the many hand arm issues that you don't want, such as carpal tunnel syndrome or cubital tunnel syndrome, and you don't want that. Be kind to your hands as far as ergonomics go, and treat them write. And if you do they're going to blog well for you for a long time to come.

Chapter 9: Introduction to Affiliate Marketing

So you've probably been wondering how you're going to monetize that blog of yours and the way you're going to do it is through a little something called affiliate marketing.

You've probably heard people tell you that you can run ads on your blog or do other things to monetize it, but don't listen to any of that mumbo-jumbo. As the real way to make money from your blog is with affiliate links. It's the way big bloggers and little bloggers alike are able to earn a real income with their blog.

So just what is affiliate marketing exactly? Well, affiliate marketing is basically when you stick a link or banner to a company's product on your blog post, and when someone buys the product through your link, you get paid a percentage.

Before you can engage in affiliate marketing, you're

first going to need to apply to affiliate programs. There are many affiliate programs out there. Big companies like Amazon have affiliate programs, as do little lesser known companies that I won't even mention because you've never even heard of them.

So how exactly do we find affiliate programs? Well, it's really simple actually, you just type in a search engine the name of a product related to your niche followed by the word "affiliate." And some affiliate programs should come up.

If your niche is so out there that no affiliate products exist for it, you might think it's all over. However, that's not entirely true, there is always something that can be found related to your niche. I've heard people tell me many times, "there are no affiliate products for my niche." And this is entirely untrue, they just weren't thinking about properly.

If you join Amazon's affiliate program, for example, you can market any product on their store, and they have a lot of products, from things like toasters, to video game consoles, to books to software. If your niche is something that someone wrote a book about, then there is at least a book that you can market.

And Amazon is not even the only affiliate program out there. There are tons.

Now, some people might get discouraged after trying to join a few affiliate programs when they realize that they were rejected. And that's normal to get rejected, especially if you're a blogger. You just have to deal with the ones who will accept you. As a precaution to getting rejected, and to optimize the chance of as many affiliate programs as possible accepting you, you want to write at least 10 to 20 blog posts first, or something, so that you have some kind of presence on the Web. And then apply to affiliate programs.

Because when you apply to affiliate programs, you have to register with them and they're going to ask you things like your name, your email, your address, your website (which means your blog), and how you plan to market their products. If your website looks like it doesn't match with their image, then they'll reject you.

However, some companies will always reject almost

everyone, because they're only looking for top influencers, and some companies will accept almost anyone, because they only care about money.

This is why you need to apply to many, many affiliate programs, so that from the ones that accept you, you then have a choice about which ones you actually choose to market on your blog.

Once a bunch of companies accepts you, you then want to log in to your affiliate dashboard, which that company should have given you a link for, and look for their banners. You want to stick around four affiliate banners in either the sidebar or footer of your blog. Why the sidebar or footer? Because these are areas that your visitors will always see, no matter which blog post of yours they read.

These banners you want to be for products that will be your blog's core products, as in the products that you always promote. Then on top of that, you want to promote other affiliate products through links in your blog posts.

When putting links in your blog posts, you don't just want to stick naked affiliate links there. Rather you want to cloak your affiliate links. Cloaking affiliate links is done in the name of professionalism, there are many WordPress plugins that can cloak your links, or you can use a link shortener like Bitly to cloak your links, which can be found at Bitly.com, that's B I T L Y dot com. There is nothing more unsightly that will ruin your blog posts than a naked affiliate link that hasn't been cloaked. So be sure to cloak your links.

So once you join a ton of affiliate programs and have banners up on your blog and have affiliate links that you can promote in your blog posts, then we're in action! And then your blog is monetized! There is nothing more you can really do once it's monetized then to throw traffic at your blog and hope some of that traffic clicks on your affiliate links and buys something.

Well, there is actually something else we can do, but we're going to get into that in a later chapter.

Chapter 10: FTC

The Federal Trade Commission, commonly referred to as the FTC should be feared, because you don't want this organization to come after you. Rather, you want to take precautions to avoid any head-on encounters with the FTC at all costs. And the best precaution to avoid such encounters from ever taking place is to be totally FTC compliant as far as affiliate marketing goes.

You see, the FTC has these rules that you must disclose your affiliate links, and you want to adhere to those rules. As you do not want to butt heads with the FTC!

You can read about their disclosure rules at:

BloggerBlogger.com/FTC

Yeah, it's a lot of stuff, I know, but if you want to earn money through your affiliate links, you'd be wise to stick to the FTC's guidelines, because if you don't, not only might the FTC come after you, but also, those affiliate programs that you spent so much time and energy to join, will ban you at the drop of a hat if they find out you were in violation of FTC guidelines.

Chapter 11: Ergonomics

This is not medical advice, but this is a recommendation, so take it as that.

When blogging, you need to make sure that you're sitting correctly and typing correctly with the correct posture. As you're going to be writing a lot, if you're posture or arms are placed in a bad position, this can lead to hand-arm issues arising, such as carpal tunnel syndrome or cubital tunnel syndrome. And you don't want those!

Thus, you want to make sure you're sitting erect in a chair with your arms down by your sides with your elbows bent in a ninety-degree angle so that your forearms are parallel with the floor.

When you type, your wrists should be in a neutral position, meaning that your thumbs should be aligned with your forearms, and your wrists should be bent slightly back.

If you are not sure what is a good ergonomically

correct position, then you should consult with a doctor who specializes in orthopedics.

Nothing could be worse for your blogging career than getting some hand-arm problem that doesn't allow you to type anymore. Therefore, you want to take this seriously.

Some people scoff at the notion of getting a hand-arm problem, and say, "I'll never get a hand-arm problem." However, I've seen enough bloggers put out of commission due to bad typing form, that I thought this was worthy of its own chapter, so if you're not sure about your posture, then you had better figure it out.

I should also say that you don't necessarily have to type out your blog posts by hand. It is perfectly acceptable to find yourself a good dictation software, and speak your blog posts. Many such softwares are built into not only computers, but also smartphones nowadays, so it's entirely possible to write your blog article with just your voice. Some of the more advanced dictation softwares even allow you to edit your work simply by using your voice alone. There is nothing wrong with speaking your blog posts.

Nothing is more valuable than your health, so I strongly urge you to blog healthily!

Chapter 12: Traffic

There are many ways one could get traffic to there blog. You'll hear some bloggers spout off about how they get traffic to their blog using social media, and I am here to tell you that you do not want to use social media to get traffic to your blog!

You want to focus on writing blog posts and only on writing blog posts. Just forget social media, you don't need it!

Now, many will disagree with me and say that social media is a great way to get exposure. That may be so, but what you're trying to do with your blog is to get your blog posts found through search engines, so that those who are searching for whatever it is that you're writing about will find your blog posts.

Social media could be used as a springboard to get some initial traffic to your blog, but ultimately it's a handicap and a diversion from what's important, you're blog posts, and so you don't need it! You know who's on social media trying to get followers for there blogs, all the small-time little bloggers who are not making a full-time income with their blog. Don't be one of them!

You see, going on social media is basically you taking on the role of a hunter, where you're hunting for followers. However, that's not the way it's supposed to be, you're a blogger, you're not supposed to hunt for your followers. Your followers are supposed to find you!

Seriously, do you honestly expect to build any long-term followers by going on social media and telling people you have a blog? Some who feel sorry for you may have a look at it, but it's actually a very poor way to build an audience. Especially from the perspective of a follower. Even if your blog does grow to be a big blog someday, and you started out by collecting followers on social media, do you really want your followers to remember that you were once so desperate for followers that you were hustling on social media to get them? Forget that! Don't play that game!

What's going to honestly get you the most traffic, is plainly and simply, writing more blog posts. So just forget all about social media.

Yes, if you missed that, simply writing more blog posts is all you need you to do in order to get more traffic to your blog. That's it! Nothing else!

It's not a quick solution, it will take time. It will take many blog posts. However, if all of your blog posts are relevant to your niche, then when someone searches for something in your niche, then ultimately, they'll find your blog at some point.

You basically want to put out so much content relevant to your niche, that the most content in that niche is coming from your blog! So anyone who searches for your topic is going to eventually find you! That's the whole key to success with blogging. It's not hunting for followers, it's putting out so much niche-related content, that all those in your niche will eventually know who you are.

It may take a hundred blog posts or it may take a thousand blog posts, but as long as you keep posting different kinds of blog posts specific to your niche, those who are into your niche will find you.

And because they found you, instead of you finding them, they're more likely to become long-term followers of your blog.

Seriously, that's all you need to do to get traffic, just stick to your posting schedule and maintain your blog. If you do only that, and you're consistent, your blog will grow, and so will your followers. It seems so simple, doesn't it? And that's because it is simple, but so few bloggers are able to consistently post, because most expect quick results. Well, it's not going to be quick. It takes time, you have to be willing to invest a year or two or more in this thing. However, the payoff is indeed worth the effort!

Now, I wouldn't exactly be telling the truth if I said all you need to do is just write blog posts, though that is 99% of it, though there is one other thing you need to do, and we're going to be covering that in the next chapter. See you there!

Chapter 13: Google Webmasters

One website in particular that you'll need to register your blog with that's going to help you to grow your blog is something called Google Webmasters. You can find them at:

Google.com/Webmasters

That's G O O G L E dot com slash W E B M A S T E R S.

Google Webmasters is all about registering your domain name with Google and ensuring that your blog posts can be easily found on Google. And there is no one better to tell you about how Google Webmasters works than Google, which is the reason I've given you a link to them.

Sure I could have written a tutorial about how to use them in this chapter, but since Google keeps updating things, it would become outdated fairly quickly. And Google already has many of their own tutorials on Google Webmasters that are more updated and better than anything that I could write, so why try and reinvent the wheel?

Now there is no rush for you to learn about Google Webmasters yet, because Google is going to automatically crawl the Web and index your blog posts anyway, even without Google Webmasters.

Therefore, you want to focus on learning about your host and WordPress as the priority.

However, once you feel you've totally mastered your host and WordPress (it shouldn't take you any more than two months to master them). Then as a next step, you want to add Google Webmasters to your continuous learning regimen.

Understanding Google Webmasters and getting your site registered with it, will really give you a leg up as far as your ability to get more traffic to your blog, so it's something you'll need to tackle eventually, but as I said, there is no rush. As it's entirely possible to grow a blog and be ultra-successful with it without ever having touched Google Webmasters. That said, figuring out Google Webmasters is definitely going to make your life as a blogger a heck of a lot easier, so you definitely should get into it when you're ready!

Chapter 14: Guest Posting

Guest posting is something you should be aware of, but it's something that I don't suggest you do unless the blog that you write a guest post for is highly relevant to what your blog is about.

What is Guest Posting?

In its purest sense, guest posting is when you write a blog post for another blog, and put a link to your blog at the end of it.

Basically, many large blogs have multiple posters, and are very hungry for more content. However, they don't just want any old piece of content, they want high-quality content, which is harder to come by nowadays then you would think. Thus, they're happy to accept any good blog posts that you submit, and have no problem letting you have some of their traffic by placing a link to your blog on a guest post.

In order to find a blog that you can write a guest post for, you'll have to basically search for your competitors in your niche, and ask them if you could write a guest post for them and what their process is for it. Each blog will have their own process for guest post submissions, and if they don't like your submission they might reject it. However, if they reject it, you can just post it to your own blog, so no harm done.

Now, I don't advise you to contact all of your competitors and ask about guest posting for their blogs. You want to make sure before asking, that their blog is much bigger and more popular than your blog, and if that's the case, then it is worth shooting over an email and asking about if you could write guest posts for their blog. I say "guest posts" and not "guest post," because if you find a blog bigger than yours that has a highly relevant audience, you'll want to write regular guest posts for them, like once a week or once a month. And these guest posts that you write will send streams of traffic from their blog to your blog for a very long time, potentially years, so it is worth doing.

However, that said, you should not count on this as being a traffic strategy, rather it should be a side strategy. And also, if that bigger blog is not really relevant to your niche, then don't ask to guest post for it. You don't need to guest post for just anyone, and you should be selective about who you guest post for.

Of course, if it's a relevant blog, and everything seems aligned with your blog, and their process for guest post submission seems clear cut and you're okay with them, then it could be a good situation for you.

Like I said, be very selective, as you don't need to guest post for anyone really, and you may even be better off just writing more blog posts for your own blog instead. Nonetheless, you should be aware that you can guest post for other blogs, and that it might be worth it in some cases, and that's why I mention it.

Chapter 15: Email Marketing

Now I did mention back in Chapter 9 that there is another way we can monetize things with your blog, and that way is called email marketing.

You only want to get into this once mastering your host, WordPress, and Google Webmasters, and once you notice a real following starting to grow on your blog, which should be apparent by people leaving comments on your blog posts or you getting some affiliate commissions from people clicking on your affiliate links and buying something. And if you've mastered those 3 things (your host, WordPress, and Google Webmasters), then you are ready for email marketing.

The concept of email marketing is rather simple, you put a form on your blog that promises some free piece of content to those who join your newsletter, and people write their email address in that form, and are then emailed that piece of content, and are now on your email list.

Once they're on your email list, you want to email them value, but at the same time, you want to email them affiliate offers. Remember all those affiliate programs that you applied for, well the ones that you didn't pick to be permanent fixtures on your blog, you should be recommending to your email list.

Once you get this system going, you are no longer simply running a blog, but you are now running a blog and newsletter. Of course, your subscribers expect you to email them things with value, and of course, you should also be emailing your list affiliate offers.

Everyone has a different approach to how to email their list, as in what percentage of their emails will be purely value, and what percentage of their emails will be affiliate offers. And to find out how this is done, I would recommend that you find some blogs and stick your email in their form, and join a bunch of email lists and see what they send you. You can start by joining my list, which you can find at:

BloggerBlogger.com

But you don't have to join my list, it's entirely up to you. You can join any list that you want.

Anyway, as far as the lists you join, you want to study their email frequency, as in how often they are sending you emails, and you want to examine what kinds of affiliate offers they send you.

Now, that free piece of content that you first have to send to your subscribers, you're probably wondering where you get that from. Well, plain and simply, you make it!

In most cases that free piece of content, which Internet Marketers call a lead magnet, is a PDF document, but it could be a video course or a free piece of software that you built, or any number of other things. It's totally up to you what it is!

But if you don't know how to build video courses, and you don't know how to build pieces of software, then probably a PDF will be the ideal lead magnet for you. And there is nothing wrong with that, as many bloggers who are quite big use PDFs as lead magnets.

The way you make your lead magnet is you first of all have to think about what your audience will find value in. And once you have an idea, you write up the content, and then export it to a PDF document, there is your lead magnet. Really simple, huh?

The next thing you need to do is set up the technical stuff, the form on your blog and the software that will manage your email list. No, you can't use Gmail, or Hotmail, or Yahoo Mail, or any kind of regular email service to manage an email list. Because you need something powerful enough that it will let you hit one button and email thousands or hundreds of thousands, or even millions of your followers at once.

The good news is, that there are many companies that can handle the whole thing for you, meaning they can help you to quickly and easily get that form set up on your blog, and set up that first email with your lead magnet and help you manage your email list. These companies are called autoresponder services.

To find out the one I recommend, just go to:

BloggerBlogger.com

And look in the Essential Resources section for Tools, and click on Best Autoresponder, and you'll find my recommendation there.

One thing though, an autoresponder service is not free, but is well worth the price. You have to think of an autoresponder as being like your mobile phone, you're going to pay a monthly bill for it, but you have an important communications tool that you can use to email your list whenever you need.

And the reality of the situation is, that you'll make more money emailing affiliate offers to your list than you will with affiliate banners on your blog or affiliate links on your blog posts. Sure you'll make some money from people who click those affiliate banners and links on your blog, but you'll make far more from your list.

Because email is a more personal experience than a blog, and so your followers are more likely to buy off of your recommendations via email. Don't ask me why, but that's just the way it is. I mean, look at any blog that's doing well, all of them have some kind of lead magnet that they're offering you to get your email on their list. Why is that? It's because they're actually making the most money off of their list. Most bloggers will not come out and say that, but that's the truth of the matter.

And the next and final piece you want to add to your continuous learning regimen is your autoresponder service. And once you have that final piece of the puzzle in place. Then you're going to do really well with your blog and with your newsletter.

This information I'm sharing with you is basically gold, so I hope you see the value in this!

Chapter 16: Blogger Lifestyle

Once your blog gets off the ground and you're making money from it, it's time for a lifestyle change.

It's a personal decision as to whether or not you want to quit your job, and I wouldn't recommend quitting your job unless your blog was earning you far more than your job is earning you.

If however, your blog was earning you the same amount as your job, I'd recommend sticking with your job for now. And the reason I recommend to stick with your job is that your income from your blog is unstable; you might be earning the same as your job this month, but who knows where that's going to be next month. If you have a bad month, where will you be? You have to consider those things before just assuming that the income from your blog is just going to come in every month. However, like I said it has to be your own decision, and you are expected to do the math on it.

Though, whether or not you quit your job, you can still live the blogger lifestyle!

So what exactly is the blogger lifestyle, you might be wondering?

Well, it's basically living life on your terms, you go where you want to go, you do what you want to do, and you always carry your laptop with you and write blog posts! Now, I get that if you are still working at your job that it's kind of hard to really live life on your own terms. However, if you have days off, then you live life on your terms during your days off. If you don't have days off, then you live life on your terms after work. Whenever you have free time, you live on your terms!

This doesn't mean that you should stop writing blog posts, because sticking to your posting schedule is a part of the terms of your life that you've previously set. So technically, you are living life on your terms by writing blog posts!

So what do you do with all that money that you earn from your blog? Well, you do whatever you want with it. I recommend playing it smart and using it to create a bright future for yourself. If you have unpaid bills, you pay your bills with it. If you like to have a coffee while writing blog posts, then you buy coffee with it. You do anything you want to do with it and make sure you save a little bit of it for those times in the future where you might have bad months. The bottom line though is that you do whatever you want to do! I mean, it's your money, you earned it, right? So no one should tell you how to spend your money, only you can decide that. Just make sure you don't squander it on frivolous things.

I've known many a blogger who did quit their job because they had a good month, and they thought that every month was going to be like that. And they bought a new computer, and new clothes, and new sunglasses, and the following month was a bad month and they wound up not being able to pay their rent and ended up homeless. They had to live out of cafes and sleep on park benches until they could have some more good months where they were then able to get back on their feet. So don't be blindsided by the money thinking that every month will be the same. You should have some money saved up and your earnings should be well above what you make at your job before you even consider quitting. And most of all, don't squander your money, but don't be afraid to spend a little and enjoy life! After all, you earned a little enjoyment for yourself spending all those hours writing blog posts! Though just promise me that when you are enjoying life, that you're enjoying life on your terms! That's important!

However, yes, you're goal should be to quit your job at one point and blog full-time. After all, that is the dream!

Chapter 17: End

Okay, we've come a long way and we've covered a lot, it's now time for you to get serious and start writing blog posts, and do all the other things that we discussed to get your blog in gear, like master your host's system, master WordPress, master Google Webmasters, and master your Autoresponder. And if you do all that, nothing can stop you! You will be an unstoppable freight train headed on track to becoming a blogging superstar.

We're talking raving fans, and nothing but first class airfare accommodations for you! And when you eat, of course, you can eat anything you want! Because you are a blogger!

The whole world caters to you, and you have options galore at your fingertips! Because you are a blogger!

And when you stop by your local favorite pizzeria, it's nothing but the best seat in the house for you, they keep it reserved for you, they keep it fresh! Fresh for you! Fresh for the blogger. Because you are a very special customer indeed! They treat you special! They treat you like the deserving fine blogger that you are! Because you are a blogger!

Yes, it's nothing but the very best for you!

However, you have a duty, and your duty is to your followers, they expect top-notch content, and they expect it in a timely fashion, so you'd better make sure that you always get out those blog posts on time! Failure to publish your blog posts on time is simply not an option!

It's funny how loyal followers so quickly turn into a rabid pack of hungry beasts if you miss a blog post!

But you get those blog posts all out on time and they're all perfect, just the way your fans like them. And your fans love you for it! Because you are a blogger!

Who wants to plug into a 9 to 5 anyway? That's not the lifestyle you want to live! You want to live life on your terms, your way. It's your way or no way! Because you are a blogger!

We're all looking forward to reading your blog

posts, we're all looking forward to seeing what you've got!

It's time to make it happen!

See you in the blogosphere!

www.ingramcontent.com/pod-product-compliance
Lightning Source LLC
Chambersburg PA
CBHW020617220526
45463CB00006B/2612